'Nor does the scenery any more affect the thoughts than the thoughts affect the scenery. We see places through our humour as through differently coloured glasses. We are ourselves a term in the equation, a note of the chord, and make discord or harmony almost at will.'

ROBERT LOUIS STEVENSON

HIGHLAND WILDERNESS

PHOTOGRAPHS BY COLIN PRIOR

TEXT BY MAGNUS LINKLATER

CONSTABLE

LONDON

FIRST PUBLISHED IN GREAT BRITAIN 1993 BY
CONSTABLE AND COMPANY LIMITED
3 THE LANCHESTERS, 162 FULHAM PALACE ROAD
LONDON W6 9ER
COPYRIGHT © 1993 TEXT BY MAGNUS LINKLATER
COPYRIGHT © 1993 PHOTOGRAPHS BY COLIN PRIOR
ISBN 0 09 471560 2

DESIGN BY IVOR CLAYDON
COLOUR SEPARATIONS BY GLOBAL COLOUR, MALAYSIA
PRINTED IN GREAT BRITAIN BY
BATH PRESS COLOURBOOKS, GLASGOW

A CIP CATALOGUE RECORD FOR THIS BOOK
IS AVAILABLE FROM THE BRITISH LIBRARY

FOR GERALDINE AND ALEXANDRA

'If one advances confidently in the direction of
his dreams and endeavours to live the life which
he has imagined, he will meet with a success
unexpected in common hours.'

THOREAU

LOCHAIN NA H'ACHLAISE AND THE BLACK MOUNT, RANNOCH MOOR, HIGHLAND.

CONTENTS

GLAS BHEINN MHOR AND GLEN ORCHY FROM BEN STARAV, GLEN ETIVE, HIGHLAND.

6

HIGHLAND WILDERNESS. IMAGES OF THE HIGHLANDS can vary as widely as the hills themselves. The photographs

in the following pages – so lovingly and skilfully created by Colin Prior – reveal a beauty that is at times ethereal. There are scenes of golden peaks, caught in the dying sun; a stretch of water scintillating under a shaft of light; dawn rising over hazy blue islands. We have called it *Highland Wilderness*, for that is the image projected here: a wild and uninhabited place, nature rampant, apparently changeless, little sign of man's intrusion. And for many people that is indeed the Highlands, an ideal to be cherished. Conserving what one writer has called that 'heroic sense of beauty and subtlety in nature' has become a vital cause in an age where everywhere the environment is threatened.

And yet, the Highlands are more complex than that, and if the true character of their wild places is to be understood, their past history and future prospects need to be explored and explained. This is not, in fact, a savage or untamed land. It is a lived-in place, one that has been vastly changed by those who have inhabited it. It has seen the trees which once covered it disappear, the people who built houses in its remote glens retreat, the sheep and deer transform its vegetation, industry alter its coast and seascape. Sometimes, looking back at the changing face of the Highlands, it seems as if only the rocks truly remain.

Recently, it has been man himself, in the form of tourists, climbers, hill-walkers and ramblers, flocking in ever-increasing numbers to breathe the air of 'the last great unexploited lung of Europe', who has posed perhaps the greatest threat of all. But threat to what? To the Highlands as they are now? To the Highlands as they might once have been? Or to the Highlands as they should be? And who is to determine precisely what that ideal state really is? Part of the strong emotional appeal this vast and rugged landscape exerts on many of us stems from an almost palpable sense of loss, a nostalgia for the days when the land was less spoiled, when people inhabited the glens, when there was what we think of as a balance between man and nature. There never was such a golden age, of course, and striving to recreate it is probably a lost cause. But to reach some kind of accommodation between the demands of the human race and those of the natural environment remains the goal of all who love the fragile landscape of the Highlands. And it is only by studying its past history that we can properly reach some understanding of how it has evolved, and how best it might be preserved.

For generations the Highlands have aroused passionate argument. Blood has been shed in their name, great suffering has been caused as their people have moved, whether forced by fellow humans, a relentless economy, or both, from the hills to the coast, and thence into exile. The past can sometimes be discerned in the form of ancient cultivation, still visible in the strips of green that run down deep straths, or the sad piles of stone which once housed human beings. Much that has been written of the Highland landscape casts it in the role of an idyll under threat, a paradise with the enemy at the gate. Its poetry is shot through with sadness, whether it is the grandness of the epic that mourns the passing of the Lords of the Isles — 'It is no joy without Clan Donald, it is no strength to be

BEINN EUNAICH AND BEINN LAOIGH, GLEN LOCHY FROM STOB DAIMH, STRATHCLYDE.

without them' – or the elegiac verses of Duncan Ban Macintyre who was alive when the sheep first came to Argyll and Perthshire and who saw the threat they posed to the Highland way of life.

Early accounts by travellers in the Highlands are less sentimental. Some, like Martin Martin, a native of Skye, who wrote of the western islands in the late seventeenth century, saw a land which was reasonably productive and a small but healthy population. But even then, he wrote, the people were desperately vulnerable to the famines which were a regular and unpredictable part of agricultural life. Others, who came from further afield, were often appalled at what they took to be the grinding poverty of Highland life. Duncan Forbes of Culloden, writing in the early part of the next century, was shocked by the crass forms of agriculture that he saw. On Tiree he wrote of the 'ridiculous processes of husbandry which almost utterly destroys the island' – corn being pulled up by the roots, weeds everywhere, straw burnt rather than used as fodder. A correspondent of *The Scotsman*, visiting the village of Torren more than a hundred years later, in 1877, wrote:

> At the top of the village, gathered in a listless way on a bit of moss land before an almost ruinous cottage were a dozen children – as squalid and as miserable as any that could be produced from the innermost dens of the Cowgate . . . puny, uncombed, blear-eyed, shivering little objects . . . This sorrowful index to the condition of the crofter forces itself very strongly on a stranger's notice as he passes through this island.

And even the beauty of the landscape failed to impress. Edward Burt, an English officer who wrote of his journeys in the north of Scotland in the 1720s, presented a decidedly unromantic view of the dark landscape through which he travelled: 'The eye penetrates far among them, and sees more particularly their stupendous bulk, frightful irregularity, and horrid gloom, made yet more sombrous by the shades and faint reflections they communicate one to another.' Dr Johnson, coming to the Highlands fifty years later, wrote off the scenery as a 'wide extent of hopeless sterility'.

It was only later, in the nineteenth century, that the mountains and the lochs began to be appreciated. Victorian trippers wrote about them, drew them, rhapsodized over their waterfalls and their deep ravines, or, as Queen Victoria put it, 'the absence of hotels and beggars'. Walter Scott's narrative poem, *The Lady of the Lake*, was a kind of nineteenth-century guidebook to the beauties of the Highland landscape. J.M.W. Turner gave the hills, glens and ruined castles a romantic touch which has survived ever since, while Landseer took them to the point of parody.

Few of those who wrote made much mention of the great changes that were affecting the landscape even then. Commercial tree-felling had already altered much of the appearance of the western Highlands and the Grampians, and Thomas Pennant, who journeyed north as early as 1769, marvelled at the prices to be made from cutting down the great Caledonian pines: Mr Farquharson of Invercauld, he wrote, had just felled 800 of them, upwards of 200 years old, and had sold them for 'five-and-twenty shillings each'. Two types of forest had once swathed the hills, though the tree-line usually stopped wherever wind and height dictated: at about 2000 feet in the eastern Grampians, dropping to below 1000 feet in the western Highlands. Everywhere there had been pinewood with birch or the broad-leafed deciduous forest of oak with birch and alder, growing densely across the Highland land mass, only thinning on the coast where salt and wind discouraged it. Deforestation, however, began almost as soon as the first prehistoric man fashioned the first flint axe and strapped it to a shaft before hacking at the nearest tree trunk. As agriculture developed properly, serious inroads were made into the thick Highland woodland. The pace quickened in the Middle Ages when forests were burnt to clear them of wolves and because they provided harbour for outlaws. Timber was cut to prepare fields for planting and to build houses and ships.

As early as the fifteenth century, the loss of woodland was being seen as a risk, and legislation was introduced in the Scots Parliament to limit tree-felling. But it had little effect, and the demands of industry, whether in foundries, which needed charcoal, or from ships and roofs which needed timber, steadily cleared what remained of the dense forest areas. In Strathspey during the eighteenth century, the York Buildings Company specialized in buying up forfeited estates, building sawmills and foundries, cutting acres of trees, and dragging them to the river where they were floated down to

BEINN LAOIGH FROM CRUACH ARDRAIN, CRIANLARICH, CENTRAL.

Kingston on the river estuary. Forty-seven ships were built there during the Napoleonic wars alone.

The great Caledonian Forest, so lamented today, had in fact largely disappeared by the eighteenth century, though remnants of it survived in the Cairngorms, Strathspey and the Great Glen. Any chance it had of natural regeneration was ended by the introduction of sheep.

Towards the middle of the eighteenth century, it was found that sheep could winter out of doors, even in the north, and with the introduction of turnips as winter fodder at the same time, the size of the herds grew, black-faced sheep being favoured over the small white-faced native breed. Steadily they replaced cattle, which were more labour-intensive, and began to alter significantly the vegetation of the uplands. It was not only that sheep cropped the tree seedlings and prevented the natural regeneration of the forest; whole areas of woodland were burnt down to provide sheep runs on a massive scale. 'Fire and tooth between them are invincible in preventing regeneration of forest,' commented the twentieth-century naturalist, Frank Fraser Darling.

For a time the burning back produced pasture for the herds which spread rapidly through the glens. But it led, just as in Brazil today, to longer-term infertility. As the chemical and organic cycle, which had always taken place beneath the cover of forest, was interrupted and brought to an end, so erosion also took place. Hill-cover was washed down from the tops, leaving the upper slopes bare and exposed; as the topsoil was carried downwards on to the flats beneath, the long natural processes which formed the peatlands were accelerated; bracken, which had been kept in check largely by the cattle whose hoofs broke and bruised it, began to spread; and the coarse grasses which had once provided grazing, but which were too tough for the sheep, now grew everywhere; heather rather than trees became the dominant vegetation.

It is ironic that much of what constitutes the beauty of the Highlands today — black-faced sheep grazing contentedly amidst the purple of the heather, the gold of the autumn bracken, scree on a Sutherland hill-slope, or the eery space of a Caithness moor — stems from changes to the natural state of things brought about largely by man. Today they would be accounted an environmental disaster.

Yet still the Highland landscape is changing. Now it is the sheep which are in retreat as the economy of hill-farming deteriorates. New forests have appeared, but instead of birch and alder, they march in serried rows of Sitka spruce, fast-growing, but uniform in outline, alien to the natural landscape and to much of its wildlife. The modern predator has become that shy, elusive and much-loved symbol of the Highlands, the red deer. The growth of the deer herds has been steady in recent years — there are said to be 300,000 now roaming the hills compared to half that number only thirty years ago. You can see them, gathered together in a corrie, or wheeling, startled, on the crest of a hill. A fine sight, but a disturbing one, for their numbers are growing too fast, so that in some areas, such as the Cairngorms, the size of the deer population (as many as 150 deer per square kilometre) has become incompatible with attempts to regenerate the forest. Short of fencing them out of specified areas, or literally decimating some of the herds (one estimate suggests that a population of 10,000 deer on the Mar Lodge/Invercauld area would have to be reduced to 1000), it is hard to see how trees can regrow naturally.

The advance of the deer is partly to do with the value of sporting rights on an estate. Deer are, after all, a significant contributor to the Highland economy in the form of venison and the high prices which visitors are prepared to pay to shoot them. This sporting income is one of the few direct tourist contributions to the cost of land management, and has helped pay for stalkers, gamekeepers and other employees in the remoter rural areas. More recently, however, the number of these local tenants has been dwindling as estates have cut back on costs, and that, aided by a succession of mild winters, has also contributed to the uncontrolled growth in the deer population. It was the skill and experience of people who had grown up on the land which traditionally kept the size of the deer herds in check. The loss of their accumulated local knowledge on such matters as culling hinds, burning heather, or controlling vermin, is a serious one.

Behind the deer comes man himself, perhaps astride a mountain-bike, resplendent in shocking pink and a plastic helmet as he pedals up an ancient drove road, churning its tracks into mud; or, bent beneath a rucksack, trudging towards another 'Munro' peak, determined to increase his total of great hills conquered; or roaring across a Highland loch on water-skis behind a launch which ploughs a deep furrow of foam across the once silent water. Just as the hand of man has been responsible for so

THE AONACH EAGACH RIDGE, GLEN COE, HIGHLAND.

many of the significant changes in the Highland landscape, so he himself now contributes the latest and perhaps most dangerous of all the threats it has faced.

But if man has often been the villain of the piece – the architect, witting or unwitting of what we see today as the wild places of the Highlands – so he has also been the victim. The people's battle for their territory, to keep it, live on it, protect and cultivate it, has been, for much of Highland history, a losing one. The land has always been poor, economically fragile, and agriculturally marginal. The history of its crofting community can be read as a continuous and often despairing attempt to hold on to land against the odds, and to cudgel a living from it in the face of disaster after disaster – whether natural or man-made.

James Hunter, author of the seminal *Making of the Crofting Community*, cites the cry of a Lewis crofter, responding to the well-meaning but misguided attempt by Lord Leverhulme in the early part of this century to offer him and his people an alternative way of farming their land:

> Come come men! This will not do! This honey-mouthed man would have us believe that black is white and white is black. We are not concerned with his fancy dreams that may or may not come true. What we want is the land – and the question I put to him now is: *will you give us the land?*

Land, its ownership, theft, retrieval, cultivation, conservation and despoliation, is the running theme throughout the history of the Highlands, and it remains at the heart of the debate about their future today. In Hunter's account, the villain of the piece is usually the landlord, rapacious, cruel and greedy, seizing every opportunity to raise profits at the expense of his people and their lives. But closer scrutiny of events suggests that it was frequently the landlord, whether clan chief or laird, who was himself the victim – forced to the brink of bankruptcy and beyond in an effort to maintain his people on land that simply did not have the resources to sustain them. Lord Macdonald spent all his capital during the potato famine of 1846 maintaining his clansmen on North Uist; Robertsons, Mackenzies of Cromarty and Lovats refused to move their people, despite conditions of great hardship, some even taking in refugees from neighbouring estates; and Macleods of Dunvegan drove themselves to penury in the mid-nineteenth century in order to keep 8000 of their tenants on the land, preferring to face ruin than let them starve. Even the second Duke of Sutherland, whose agents, James Loch and Patrick Sellar, were responsible for some of the most brutal of the clearances under the much-vilified first Duke early in the nineteenth century, spent £8000 (say, £250,000 at today's value) on famine relief.

It was during this century that the general shift of the Highland population from the hills and glens to the coastal regions took place. There, fishing and kelping – gathering seaweed which, when incinerated, provided potash and soda for the manufacture of glass, soap and dye – helped for a time to supplement the meagre living that was to be got from the much poorer land at sea-level. For about fifty years kelping afforded employment for thousands of people (3000 in Orkney alone), albeit for desperately low wages. But as so often with the Highland economy, developments elsewhere undermined the industry. Cheaper substitutes were found, and the abolition of duties on imported material made the transport south of kelp unviable. Fishing, in particular the herring industry, lasted longer, with the great expansion of the herring fleets in the mid-nineteenth century offering employment to crofters, both men and womenfolk, not only for catching, but for curing the fish. For a time it seemed as if fishing would be the saving of the Highlands since there were summer jobs to be

13

had as well as winter employment on the boats; but this industry too fell victim, partly to its own success as record catches drove prices down, but also to the imposition of import duties, this time by European countries anxious to protect their own markets. In 1887, it was estimated that about £40,000 was lost to the crofting population of Lewis alone because of the slump in the herring industry, and the average wage brought back from the east-coast fishings, where the Lewismen went for work in the summer, fell from £20 or £30 in the early 1880s to just £1 or £2.

The introduction of the potato as the staple diet of the Highlander in the 1740s meant that there was an ability to weather the occasional failures of the grain harvest and support the population at a reasonably steady level until the first appearance of the potato disease a century later. Massive famine relief operations sent north from Glasgow, Edinburgh and London meant that relatively few died, but again the vulnerability of the local economy was exposed.

Despite all these setbacks, the population of the Highlands climbed in the first half of the nineteenth century, and was actually higher at the end of it than it had been at the beginning. The worst periods of population drift did not take place during the clearances, the decline of the kelping industry, the slump in the herring trade, or the potato famine, but later, during the depression years of the present century. As the historian T.C. Smout amongst others has pointed out, seven of the Highlands and Islands counties actually reached their historic peaks of population during the first half of the nineteenth century, when the clearances were taking place. Between 1851 and 1891 there was only an 11 per cent fall in the Highlands, but an 18 per cent fall in the rest of Scotland. And in the 1880s, the massive four-volume Napier Commission report concluded that there were still too many people in the Highlands with too little land to support them. The real drain of people away from the crofts into the cities or exile took place in the years between 1851 and 1931, a period when it was virtually impossible under Scottish law to evict a Highland crofter from his holding. From a peak of just under 400,000 people in 1850 throughout the crofting counties (including Orkney and Shetland), the numbers fell to below 300,000 in the 1930s. From making up 20 per cent of the total Scottish population, the Highland proportion has dropped to barely 6 per cent today. The downward trend has been partly reversed in the latter part of the present century, helped by modern industries such as nuclear energy, oil, fish-farming and tourism, but it has never again reached its nineteenth-century pinnacles.

Arguably, the Highland economy in the nineteenth century, was never a seriously viable one. The industries and crops which supported the people did so only because conditions of what today would be called poverty were accepted. As living standards rose elsewhere, in the lowlands and the cities of the mainland, so the disparity between the Highlands and the rest grew wider. Professor Smout quotes a contemporary observer, W.P. Alison, as far back as 1847, saying: 'When we find a population living chiefly on potatoes and reduced to absolute destitution, unable to purchase other food when the potato crop fails, we have at once disclosed to us the undeniable fact, that that population is redundant.' That is an extreme view, but it found an echo when a British government official, confronting the disaster of the potato famine in the 1840s, concluded: 'No resource could suggest itself more naturally, under these circumstances, than the removal of the people, bodily, from the land which is no longer adequate to support them.'

Nevertheless, the tenacity of the crofting community in sticking to the land, despite adverse conditions, has been one of its salient characteristics. 'Crofters have always considered the hardships that are the unavoidable consequences of their natural environment to be more bearable than those that have resulted from human action,' wrote Hunter. Successive governments, despite that earlier view, have therefore tried to find ways of ensuring that they could stay on the land and gain a living from it. From Gladstone's Crofters Act of 1886 to the establishment of the Highlands and Islands Development Board – later Highlands and Islands Enterprise – in 1965, there have been efforts to reverse the decline in the Highland economy, with varying degrees of success. Some imported industries, like aluminium-smelting and paper-mills, offered great hope, but fell victim to changing economic conditions. Others, like oil, have brought relative prosperity and higher employment to some areas, such as those round the Cromarty Firth, in Orkney and in Shetland. But they have not settled doubts about longer-term prospects. Fish-farming, probably the biggest boom industry in the Highlands, has spread rapidly around the coast, and though fears have been expressed about the pollution it can cause to the sea bed, and the way its cages detract from the unspoilt beauty of Highland sea lochs, there is no doubt that it has come to the aid of many an isolated community.

Increasingly, however, thoughts have turned to maintaining the Highlands as an area of outstanding natural beauty, and valuing that as one of its principal assets. To do that as well as ensuring that the region continued to support people has been a major consideration. 'Until the Highland problem is looked upon as social rather than economic,' wrote Frank Fraser Darling in 1938, 'it is to be feared that we can expect little improvement.' Today, the social and the economic are inseparable, but the principle remains the same.

The two aims – finding employment for people and preserving the environment – are by no means incompatible. But striking the balance has taxed some of the best minds brought to bear on the problem over the past century. One extreme view was voiced by a policy adviser to the Prime Minister in 1979, as recorded by Professor Alastair Hetherington of Stirling University:

> Does it matter if Ardnamurchan, Applecross and West Sutherland become uninhabited? If people choose to live in such places, why shouldn't they pay something closer to the economic cost of the services they require? Why should taxpayers in Manchester, Derby, Nottingham and Southampton have to subsidize them? Will anything be lost if those areas revert to wilderness?

That position, perhaps not intended entirely seriously, would fall down on several obvious counts. Firstly, no civilized modern state can simply abandon one part of its territory and allow its standard of living to drift hopelessly behind another's, without causing a basic social instability. And secondly, if that territory happens to be itself a priceless asset, it requires nurturing rather than neglect.

It was John Muir, one of the first and greatest of conservationists, a Scot from Dunbar in East Lothian, who first proposed a way forward for such territories. He had seen the destruction of the redwood and pine forests of the High Sierra in California, and realized that if their remnants were to be preserved, then special areas, protected by man for man, would have to be created. The National Park at Yosemite is his most famous legacy, but he left too a notion of how the wilderness he loved so much should be regarded. As John Morton Boyd, first Director of the Nature Conservancy Council, put it: '. . . not a place of savagery to be tamed, nor of waste to be transformed for profit, nor a curse to be shunned and feared, but a sacred place of natural renewal and adjustment and a civilizing influence upon all mankind.'

Living up to that ideal has been a test for many of the twentieth-century ecologists who followed Muir. His principal disciple in Scotland was Fraser Darling, whose *West Highland Survey* is still a classic of keen observation and shrewd analysis. But his ideas were officially ignored by the Scottish Office which had commissioned him to write it. He was perhaps too idealistic in suggesting that the Highlands could be significantly repopulated, to establish a working environment for people living in harmony with the wildlife he loved. And he was perhaps too uncompromising in his conclusion that '. . . the bald unpalatable fact is emphasized that the Highlands and Islands are largely a devastated terrain, and that any policy which ignores this fact cannot hope to achieve rehabilitation.'

Nevertheless, many of his ideas have survived, and they have influenced the thinking that led to the establishment of such bodies as the Nature Conservancy Council, certainly the most important of the post-war conservation organizations. One of the pre-Conservancy papers produced along the Fraser Darling line concluded:

> It is useless to declare an area a nature reserve and then to leave it to its own devices. Lack of adequate control speedily defeats the objects for which the reserve was intended. If nature reserves are to be successful, it is imperative that they be managed scientifically, and that they be used as observational areas for gaining new knowledge about plant and animal fluctuations under natural conditions.

Such ideas should, in Fraser Darling's view, have led to the establishment of national parks in Scotland. There was a time in the 1950s when five designated areas, examined by a National Parks Committee, could have been acquired for around £3.5 million or just 50p an acre. Nevertheless, though national parks were established in England and Wales, they have never been introduced in Scotland. This may have been partly because they were thought unnecessary, partly because of cost, and partly perhaps because there was a view that the bureaucracy and land management that went with them did not suit the freedom and wildness of the Scottish Highlands. The failure to establish national parks was, in Fraser Darling's view, a lost opportunity. 'Scotland has been left as the only nation of any consequence, civilized or not, that is without a system of national parks,' he wrote. '. . . planning, land apportionment and landscaping are being neglected to the detriment of the working capital of the Highlands, which is its scenery.'

Instead, decisions which affect the Highlands are made at different levels by the Scottish Office, local authorities, private landlords, charitable trusts, voluntary bodies, government agencies such as Scottish Natural Heritage or Highlands and Islands Enterprise, and organizations like the Scottish National Trust and the Royal Society for the Protection of Birds, which between them own some of the most famous areas of outstanding natural beauty. Opinions vary as to how well they administer their heritage, and whether their plans for the future will work. But there has at least been recently a better awareness of the need for a co-ordinated policy. Instead of running warfare between those who own the land and those who wish to enjoy it, an alliance, albeit an uneasy one, has begun to emerge.

At the same time the challenge to be faced has grown steadily more daunting as the number of people demanding access to the once remote areas of the north has increased. 'Visitor pressure' is the current jargon, and though recreation and the encouragement of ever more sightseers are seen as the key to local employment and the future of the economy, the growth in numbers poses, in some areas at least, a real threat to the very environment the visitors have come to enjoy.

Most people who come to the Highlands have in their minds an idea of wildness, and for some it is fixed by the memories of a particular day. I have two pictures that stand out. One is of Kintail, on a day of searing heat in June, high on the green hills that form the Five Sisters, where we came across a spring, bubbling unexpectedly below the tops; the water was clear and icy cold, and I can still

DAWN, OLDSHOREMORE BAY, KINLOCHBERVIE, SUTHERLAND.

remember the first sharp taste of it. The second memory is of lying amongst blaeberries on Stac Polly, looking down on to Loch Lurgainn, where the surface was of an almost unimaginable turquoise.

In neither of these memories can I recall the intrusion of other people. Empty hills, deserted beaches, open waters, these were the norm. Yet now, Stac Polly displays a deep and angry scar, chiselled cruelly into its southern slope, where the climbers mount in single file; and you cannot reach the tops of the Five Sisters on a summer's afternoon without jostling your way past fellow-walkers. The nearer the centres of population, the greater, of course, the threat. Loch Lomond, pleasure-ground for generations of Glaswegians, is probably the best case in Scotland for a specially designated national park, for here the muddy tracks on the hills, trodden by thousands of walkers, the roar of the speedboats on the loch, the caravans, the litter and the sheer weight of people, impose almost intolerable burdens on the natural surroundings. Without protective measures, such places might simply become rural slums.

To confront this challenge the Nature Conservancy Council, for long regarded in Scotland as an autocratic body, run from Peterborough in England, was merged in 1992 with the Countryside Commission and replaced by the Scottish Natural Heritage Agency, headed by the broadcaster and naturalist, Magnus Magnusson, and sited in Scotland. It regards itself primarily as a facilitating body, bringing together the many vested interests in the Highlands, and trying to get them to work together in the interests of conservation – 'getting hold of the people who manage the ground', as Magnusson puts it. Whether it can achieve its ends simply by gentle persuasion remains to be seen, and there is no lack of sceptics on this score. They would argue that an organization without teeth, without the ability to intervene and direct land use, cannot properly protect our natural heritage. Magnusson believes that intervention is the last resort, and argues that co-operation is far more effective. He says that the objective must be to have people living and working on the land if the Highlands are to survive. He recoils from the word 'wilderness' because it implies an area emptied of people. 'If you don't have people on the ground, you can't manage it,' he says.

Increasingly, the once-vilified estate owner has become a key figure in the future of the Highlands, an asset to be cherished, almost an endangered species himself, since it is he who can help maintain the balance of nature that hill-walkers and nature-lovers have come to expect. If the deer are to be kept back so that the trees can grow; if the rivers are to be protected so that the salmon thrive; if the moors are to be guarded from predators so that bird life flourishes; if all this is to be achieved, then there must be someone to employ the people to do it. And while landlords will naturally have a keen self-interest – the maintenance of a sporting estate for private pleasure or for profit – and while they may not be overjoyed by ramblers trekking across their hills, their interests and those of the naturalist often, surprisingly, combine.

As Sir Robert Grieve, first Chairman of the Highlands and Islands Development Board, puts it:

Today, one could reasonably point out that there is the growth of an almost universal movement of ordinary folk towards the view of the sporting people of the upper classes in the last few generations; in short, the curious effect of the contemporary conservationist movement (or some interpretations of it) is to make the preservationist Highland landlord more acceptable, to urban people at least, for the first time in five or six generations.

That is not, of course, the only way of preserving the wild areas. Some, like the Torridon estate in Wester Ross, owned by the Scottish National Trust, are managed with visitors in mind, hill-paths carefully created and maintained, the great sandstone peaks mapped and explained to the many hundreds of enthusiasts who climb, or attempt to climb them. Others, like the Rothiemurcus estate near Aviemore, privately owned, but working closely with Scottish Natural Heritage, cater specifically for the kind of visitor who may never have climbed a hill in anger, but who still wants to see and enjoy wildlife and unspoilt country, preferably under the watchful eye of an estate ranger. Still others, like Knoydart, are relatively hard for the average tourist to reach, and cater more for the enthusiastic climber who knows the hills and is aware of the threats they face. A recent survey amongst these latter revealed that more than 70 per cent would be prepared to pay a so-called 'boot tax' – a charge paid for the privilege of climbing in certain areas. Whether schemes like this could ever be a serious source of income in the Highlands remains to be seen.

Some places are hardy, rugged and perfectly capable of resisting the impact of hill-walkers and climbers. Torridon would probably fall into this category. So too would Glencoe, managed by the National Trust for Scotland and watched over by its mentor, the mountaineer Hamish MacInnes, who is a great encourager of visitors. Others are vulnerable. The Cairngorms, for instance, are regarded by the naturalists Desmond Nethersole-Thompson and Adam Watson as desperately in need of protection from those who regularly invade them. It is ten years since they wrote these words:

> The challenge we face in the Cairngorms is how best to decide between immediate and long-term priorities. Nothing is yet irretrievably lost . . . But the wonderful tops and plateaux are already at greater risk than at any time since the last ice age. And down in the valleys many of the grandest relics of the Old Caledonian Forest are steadily disappearing and heading for extinction. Time is short, and fast running out.

It would be hard to maintain that matters have greatly improved since that statement was made, though major steps have been taken to protect specific areas of outstanding natural interest.

The special category of Sites of Special Scientific Interest is given to those areas where there are rare plants, natural woodland, unspoilt tracts of moss or peatland, or other natural formations that need saving, not just from intrusive tourists, but from commercially minded estate-owners anxious to plough or plant on them. Large sums of money are regularly paid out in compensation to prevent that happening, with the result that 14 per cent of the Highlands is now designated as SSSIs, with another 20 per cent falling into the lesser category of National Scenic Areas. Quite how successful this policy has been, is doubtful. Making sure the SSSIs are effectively managed and keeping an eye on them year after year is demanding, bureaucratic and expensive. It also tends to create museum pieces out of parts of our natural heritage, rather than incorporating them into the general management of the Highlands. The aim these days is to move away from SSSIs, and Magnus Magnusson believes that if the voluntary principle of co-operation which his agency is so keen to foster can be made to work,

then he would like to see a time when designating bits of land in this way ceases to be necessary. There is, however, some nervousness about the prospect of forthcoming European legislation. This would override domestic laws and insist that special sites, which might number as many as 50 per cent of the existing SSSIs, be more aggressively managed and protected than they are at present.

That is for the future. For the time being, rather than national parks, the idea is to have National Heritage Areas, which rely for their protection on voluntary agreements instead of draconian legislation. The current phrase, 'sustainable development', first coined by the World Commission on Environment and Development, is now used to describe the way in which the natural habitat of the Highlands can be maintained, not as wilderness areas, bereft of human habitation, but as places

SUNRISE, CASTLE HILL, LOCH MORLICH, HIGHLAND.

where development and the environment can go hand in hand. As one recent report on the future of the Highlands puts it:

> The environment will no more improve if people go away or communities are impoverished than if it is swamped by hordes of visitors.

Or, as Magnusson says:

> The greatest renewable resource of all is man. Scotland is nothing without its people. But the people of Scotland are nothing without Scotland – and our aim must be to ensure that this Scotland of ours continues to be worth living in. The heritage and stewardship of nature is ours.

There will never be a consensus of view about the Highlands, about how they should look, be lived in, be nurtured or preserved. We will continue to see them through Robert Louis Stevenson's different coloured glasses – and man himself will always be a term in the equation. But at the same time we cannot simply stand back and allow these wild places to be eroded, whether by commercial exploitation, by pollution, by uncontrolled tourism or by simple neglect. Each area demands an approach geared to its particular needs. In some places tourism needs positively to be encouraged to sustain a local economy; it must, however, be sensibly and imaginatively managed rather in the way that Switzerland exploits but at the same time sustains its natural assets. In other places, there needs to be a policy of more aggressive intervention to save the land from the mass influx of people, or to control the deer population; here, the case for national parks, first argued more than fifty years ago, is likely to become irresistible.

In the vast majority of the places revealed in these pages, the essential approach must be to find a means of balancing interests, whether those of the crofter, the laird, the tourist or the manager of local industry. There will be no magic solution, and there will be inevitable set-backs as economic trends which are more likely to have their origins in London or Brussels rather than Fort William or Ullapool have their effect. But if the lessons of the past can be absorbed and understood, and if the consistency of land management which the Highlands so desperately needs can be brought to bear, then their natural heritage stands a real chance of being saved for the future – with man playing a central role.

The first step in guarding that heritage is awareness of its value, and the photographs that follow show just how much is at stake. In taking us from the Southern Highlands to the far North-West, Colin Prior and his remarkable images reveal a landscape of rare but fragile beauty which demands to be protected, cherished and renewed.

THE SOUTHERN HIGHLANDS. STRETCHING FROM THE LINE OF THE FORTH-CLYDE CANAL across the centre of

Scotland, north to the River Awe and Glen Orchy as far as the bleakness of Rannoch Moor and the grandeur of Loch Tummel, this area includes some of the best loved and most visited of all Scotland's hill country as well as some of its most remote peaks.

To the south, Ben Lomond, overlooking Loch Lomond, is the most southerly of Scotland's 'Munros' – hills over 3000 feet – and is the most popular and most often climbed of all the major Scottish peaks. Today it is a day's outing from Glasgow. But to early climbers it contained more than an element of mystery and danger, 'exciting a degree of surprise, arising almost to terror', according to an eighteenth-century account.

West from Ben Lomond, at the top of Loch Long, is the village of Arrochar, and it is north and west from here, in the mountains known as the Arrochar Alps, that some of the most popular climbing in the whole of Scotland takes place. Peaks like Beinn Arthur (The Cobbler), Beinn Narnain, Beinn Ime, A'Chrois, Ben Vane and Ben Vorlich are famous for their spectacular buttresses and their fearsome rock faces, coated with lichen, slippery when wet, and sufficiently challenging for some of the world's best mountaineers.

Further west, between Loch Goil and Loch Fyne, both of which reach deep into the wilds of Argyll, is Beinn an Lochain, south of the road which passes through Glen Croe and Glen Kinglas on its way to Inveraray. It is the highest mountain in the Ardgoil area, its twin peaks a mass of crags and gullies, plunging down to Loch Restil. Much of the land here is the Argyll Forest Park, managed by the Forestry Commission, and is well covered by larch and spruce with a scattering of Scots pine. The long level ridge of Binnein an Fhidleir opens up long vistas across Loch Fyne.

The West Highland Way, which follows the east shore of Loch Lomond and takes the adventurous walker all the way to Fort William, also makes the transition from the rich green of Argyll to the hardier terrain of the western Grampians. Through Glen Falloch, it skirts the hills of Crianlarich, south-east of the town, before heading north and west. Here the hills are grass-covered and evenly weathered, the largest, like Ben More, giving superb views across half of Scotland.

Further north, through Strathfillan, woods of silver birch and some rare Caledonian pines give way to more forbidding hills and bleak moorland. The mountains here form a twisting ridge from Beinn Dorain to Beinn a'Chreachain, overlooking the West Highland railway as it snakes north to Bridge of Orchy, taking its privileged passengers through some of the most breathtaking scenery that British Rail can offer its customers.

The rail line divides at Tyndrum, and the western spur heads for Oban, parallel with the road along Glen Lochy and underneath the great twin tops of Ben Lui, one of the grandest mountains in the Southern Highlands, source of the River Tay, where the Nature Conservancy (now Scottish Natural Heritage) has established a small nature reserve, famous for its alpine plants, on the north-west side. Ben Lui lies on an almost straight east-west line between two Ben Mores – one to the east, already mentioned, and another, further off to the west, on the island of Mull, from where the whole of this jagged western coast can be seen. To the north there is the Ardnamurchan peninsula and Morvern, separated off by the deep inlet of Loch Linnhe; to the south there is Jura, Islay, the Mull of Kintyre and the Kyles of Bute.

On a bright autumn day, with the bracken golden on Ben More, Mull presents as glorious a sight as anything on Scotland's western seaboard. It is a tourist's delight, and in the summer its cottages and hotels do brisk business. But, despite the richness of its soil, Mull is sadly under-populated, its local communities diminished, its economy increasingly held back by high transport costs. Other islands, like Seil, Lung, or the little slate island of Easdale, are sufficiently close to the mainland and the quarrying operations there to support a reasonable number of people, but with the decline of local farming the future prospects for these island communities are uncertain.

24

ICEFLOW, BEINN AN LOCHAIN, GLEN CROE, STRATHCLYDE.

Dawn light, Beinn Dorain, Bridge of Orchy, Strathclyde.

28

SUNRISE, BEN LOMOND, LOCH LOMOND, STRATHCLYDE.

ERRATICS, AND BEINN EUNAICH, GLEN LOCHY, STRATHCLYDE.

MOONRISE, CRIANLARICH HILLS, STRATH FILLAN, CENTRAL.

34

THE ARGYLL PEAKS FROM THE SUMMIT OF CRUACH ARDRAIN, CRIANLARICH, CENTRAL.

ALPENGLOW, BEN MORE, STOB BINNIEN AND CRUACH ARDRAIN, STRATH FILLAN, CENTRAL.

DAWN, KYLES OF BUTE, LOCH RIDDON, TIGHNABRUACH, STRATHCLYDE.

INVERARY FROM ST CATHERINES, LOCH FYNE, STRATHCLYDE.

42

GALE-FORCE WAVES, ELLANBEICH, EASDALE SOUND, EASDALE, STRATHCLYDE.

LOCH LINNIE AND THE MORVEN PENINSULA FROM BEINN A' BHETHIR, BALLACHULLISH, HIGHLAND.

BINNEIN AN FHIDHLEIR, GLEN KINGLAS ACROSS LOCH FYNE, STRATHCLYDE.

47

SILVER BIRCH AND CALEDONIAN PINES, RIVER FALLOCH, CENTRAL.

CAIRNDOW LOCH FYNE FROM CLACHAN, GLEN FYNE, STRATHCLYDE.

WINTER LIGHT AND CATTLE, CROFTAMIE, CENTRAL.

THE VIEW NORTH FROM THE SUMMIT OF BEN LOMOND, CENTRAL.

BEINN ARTHUR 'THE COBBLER' AND BEINN NARNAIN, ARROCHAR, STRATHCLYDE.

CENTRAL HIGHLANDS.

RANNOCH MOOR was once a vast pine forest. Today, bare of trees, it is a strange, bleak peatland, its dark little lochs, tussocks and boulders giving it the appearance of a lunar landscape. It is the gateway to what can loosely be described as the Central Highlands, an area bounded by the Great Glen to the north and guarded by the stern peaks of Ben Alder, Schiehallion and Ben Lawers to the east. From the south, Rannoch Moor is approached by the Black Mount and Loch Tulla, and is home to a rich variety of bird life, including dunlin and golden plover, as well as that rare plant the Rannoch rush, which is found nowhere else. This is the open prelude to the great peaks of the Glen Coe Boundary Fault, and the first sight of these daunting shapes on the horizon as you approach them from the south is always an awesome one. They rear up in the distance, gaining distinctive shapes as you get nearer, forming a fortress-wall around the southern side of the glen which was home for four centuries to the small but stubborn clan of the Glencoe MacDonalds. Its mountains, running north and west, are Buachaille Etive Beag and Buachaille Etive Mor, Beinn Fhada, Bidian nam Bian and Stob Coire nan Lochan. The tower at its summit is the top of the Crowberry Ridge, perhaps the most famous rock climb in Scotland. These gullies and buttresses are a climber's paradise, though difficult to reconnoitre, and dangerous in poor weather. The northern wall of Glencoe, round which Colonel Hamilton brought 400 soldiers – arriving too late because of a snowstorm on the Devil's Staircase – to take his part in the massacre on the morning of 13 February 1692, is Aonach Eagach, a long and formidable ridge, whose highest peak is Meall Dearg. The rock formations of Glencoe are extraordinary, dark and red, formed of porphyritic lavas which have welled up and subsided, leaving scars and fissures like the skin on an old man's face. But though the glen, in harsh weather, can be grim, it has, in summer, a gentle feel to it, with its pasture-land, its waters, and its clumps of woodland reminding us that this was once a well-populated place which had clustered villages, strips of cultivated land, cattle and sheep.

To the south-west is Glen Etive, a more wooded area, where most of the Glencoe people escaped at the height of the massacre, leading down to Loch Etive and the impressive peak of Ben Cruachan. In the opposite direction, north-east, beyond the Mamore Forest, rears an even more formidable mountain, the hunched shoulder that is Ben Nevis.

54

LOCHAIN NA H'ACHLAISE AND THE BLACK MOUNT, RANNOCH MOOR, HIGHLAND.

'SEA OF CLOUD' AND THE GLENCOE PEAKS FROM STOB GHABHAR, HIGHLAND.

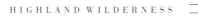

58

SRON NA CREISE, BUACHAILLE ETIVE MOR, RANNOCH MOOR, HIGHLAND.

CALEDONIAN PINE, LOCH TULLA AND STOB GHABHAR, INVERORAN, HIGHLAND.

BEINN TOAIG AND CLACH LEATHAD, LOCH TULLA, GLEN ORCHY, HIGHLAND.

BEINN FHADA AND STOB COIRE NAN LOCHAN FROM AM BODACH, GLENCOE, HIGHLAND.

ROWAN AND BIRCH, LAIRIG GARTAIN, GLEN ETIVE, HIGHLAND.

BIDEAN NAM BIAN AND THE GLENCOE PEAKS FROM THE SUMMIT OF BEN STARAV, GLEN ETIVE, HIGHLAND.

BEINN ACHALADAIR, BEINN AN DOTHAIDH AND BEINN DORIAN. LOCH TULLA, INVERORAN, HIGHLAND.

CALEDONIAN PINE, HOLLY AND SILVER BIRCH, ROBBER'S WATERFALL, GLEN ETIVE, HIGHLAND.

74

STOB COIRE NAN LOCHAN AND THE AONACH EAGACH RIDGE FROM BIDEAN NAM BIAN, GLENCOE, HIGHLAND.

STOB COIRE NAN LOCHAN AND RAINBOW, RIVER COE, GLENCOE, HIGHLAND.

BUACHAILLE ETIVE MOR AND RIVER ETIVE, GLEN ETIVE, HIGHLAND.

RANNOCH MOOR AND THE BLACK MOUNT PEAKS, HIGHLAND. (WINTER)

RANNOCH MOOR AND THE BLACK MOUNT PEAKS, HIGHLAND. (AUTUMN)

BEINN FHADA AND BUACHAILLE ETIVE MOR FROM STOB COIRE NAN LOCHAN, GLENCOE, HIGHLAND.

BEN NEVIS AND THE MAMORE FOREST, GLEN NEVIS, HIGHLAND.

RIPPLE REFLECTIONS, RIVER ETIVE, GLEN ETIVE, HIGHLAND.

MOONRISE, 'PAP OF GLENCOE', LOCH LEVEN, HIGHLAND.

EASTERN HIGHLANDS.

THAT THE CAIRNGORMS have been proposed as a world heritage site is not surprising. They are unique in Britain, indeed in Europe, both for the open mountain wilderness they present and for the richness of their wild life. The best approach is from the south, along the A9, where, beyond Blair Atholl, the transition from the smooth hills of agricultural Perthshire to the rugged grandeur of the Grampians is sudden and spectacular. To the east, the first of the range to be seen are Beinn Dearg and Beinn a Ghlo, part of the Atholl Forest, then, as the road and the railway which shadows it snake deeper into Badenoch, over the Drumochter Pass at 1500 feet, the true Cairngorms are opened up — mountains like Cairn Gorm itself, Ben MacDui and Ben Avon. To the north lie the Mondhliath Mountains, Strathspey and the Forest of Moy, but it is to the south that some of the great hill-walking areas, like Lairig Ghru, Lochnagar, Lairig an laoigh, Glenfeshie and Glen Tilt, are to be found. Too often the old drove roads are muddy and eroded by the sheer weight of walking boots, but there is still a vivid sense of wildness and isolation to be experienced.

The easiest access is probably from Aviemore, striking east by Loch Morlich to the foothills of Cairngorm; Glenmore Lodge is a favourite departure point, and it was from here that the late Eric Beard set up something of a record by climbing the four highest Cairngorms, and arriving back at the lodge in four and a half hours; another approach, via the A93 north to Braemar, takes the walker to the Spittal of Glenshee, a delight for climbers and skiers alike; there are easier walks further east, up Glen Esk to Tarfside and towards Lochnagar.

Some estates, like Rothiemurcus, are managed with walkers and tourists in mind. Some, like Atholl, Mar, Invercauld and Braemar, are sporting estates. Others, like Abernethy Forest, owned by the Royal Society for the Protection of Birds, and the St Cyrus Nature Reserve, towards the eastern coast, are conserved for wildlife. The range of vegetation, alpine and sub-alpine, pine forests and birch wood, heath and grassland, is vast, supporting a wide variety of animal and bird life. Rivers like the Feshie, the Spey, the Ythan, the Avon, the North Esk and the Dee provide spectacular scenery and equally spectacular sport.

The Cairngorms present one of the great tests for conservationists. Their wildness is their greatest asset, but it is increasingly at risk from those who wish to visit them. Plans to purchase the Mar Lodge estate for the nation seem, for the moment, to have foundered. Attempts to control the deer and regenerate woodland are making but slow progress.

THE MONADHLIATH MOUNTAINS, NEWTONMORE, HIGHLAND.

The Lairig Ghru and the Cairngorm Mountains, Rothiemurchus Forest, Grampian.

EARLY MORNING, ST. CYRUS NATURE RESERVE, GRAMPIAN.

DERRY CAIRNGORM AND BEINN MHEADHOIN, CAIRNGORM MOUNTAINS, GRAMPIAN.

BEINN MHEADHOIN AND STACAN DUBHA, LOCH AVON, CAIRNGORM MOUNTAINS, GRAMPIAN.

MEALL A BUACHAILLE, ROTHIEMURCHUS FOREST, CAIRNGORM, HIGHLAND.

104

MOONRISE OVER A' MHARCONAICH AND AN TORC, PASS OF DRUMOCHTER, HIGHLAND.

SUNSET, CASTLE HILL, LOCH MORLICH, HIGHLAND.

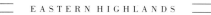

RIVER NORTH ESK, GLEN ESK, EDZLL, GRAMPIAN.

CREAG MEAGAIDH AND COIRE ARDAIR, MOY FOREST, GLEN SPEAN, HIGHLAND.

112

LOCHNAGAR AND WHITE MOUNTH, RIVER DEE, BRAEMAR, GRAMPIAN.

SANDS OF FORVIE, YETHAN ESTUARY, NEWBURGH, GRAMPIAN.

EBB TIDE AT DAWN, ST. CYRUS, GRAMPIAN.

RIVER NORTH ESK AND THE ROCKS OF SOLITUDE, GLEN ESK, GRAMPIAN.

THE NORTH-WESTERN HIGHLANDS.

IF A HIGHLAND WILDERNESS can be said truly to exist, then this is it. Running from the hills of Sutherland and Wester Ross down to the Great Glen, it is, for some, the spiritual centre of the Highlands. Certainly, poets like Norman MacCaig and Sorley Maclean, naturalists like Frank Fraser Darling, or writers like Gavin Maxwell, have cherished the north-western Highlands above all others: 'Nowhere in all the West Highlands and Islands have I seen a place of so intense and varied beauty in so small a compass,' wrote Maxwell of his beloved Sandaig.

There is no better way of starting than taking the train from Dingwall to Kyle of Lochalsh, from the rich farmland of Easter Ross, through moor and mountain country of rare beauty, clattering past tiny stations like Achnasheen, following the course, first of the River Bran, then the River Carron, until the sea opens up and the Cuillin Hills become the middle ground of the most heart-wrenching view in Scotland. To the south, there are peaks which anyone can climb, around Glen Shiel and Kintail – the Five Sisters, The Saddle, Beinn Fhada, Beinn Sgritheall, Faochag – and sea-bays of shimmering beauty – Morar, Arisaig, Glenelg, Inverie – where even today you can walk, undisturbed by anything other than a questioning seal. To the north, beyond the Applecross peninsula, lies Loch Torridon, with its hills of strange Torridonian sandstone, weathered and heroic. The heights of Liathach and Beinn Eighe are much-loved by climbers, but it is still possible, even in midsummer and however crowded the car-parks, to find yourself alone within minutes as you strike out for some distant corrie. Torridon is owned by the National Trust for Scotland, which maintains its paths well. Further north,

RIVER BRAN, STRATHBRAN FOREST, ACHNASHEEN, HIGHLAND.

at Loch Maree, Scottish Natural Heritage takes over, equally meticulous in its care. If you have chosen to drive from the east, rather than go by rail, you approach Loch Maree by Kinlochewe, opening up a sudden view to the west, with Beinn Eighe to the left, Slioch to the right, and in front of you the loch, the sea and distant Harris. It is as unexpected as it is spectacular. The road west to Gairloch now takes the motorist past the head of Loch Ewe, then circles back on itself, until it is running east past Gruinard Bay, down Little Loch Broom and under the magnificent escarpment of An Teallach – 'Liathach's only rival', according to the mountaineer Tom Weir. Looking east from here, across the Dundonnel Forest, there is another peak, Beinn Dearg. Frank Fraser Darling wrote of this:

> When the snow is down, an east wind blowing hard, the sky leaden and the tops partly hidden, Beinn Dearg and An Teallach roar to one another from the unapproachable country of their summits. I do not know what causes this deep song in the hills . . . I am inclined to place [it] in the same category of sounds as the phenomenon of the singing sands.

North again, past the prosperous tourist and fishing town of Ullapool, and Sutherland takes over. The mountains of Suilven, Stac Polly, Canisp, Quinag, and Ben More Assynt, are so distinctive, so full of unexpected shape and character, that you can never weary of them. They have, as Tom Weir puts it, 'a dignity out of all proportion to their size'. Glacier-formed, they were once covered by pine forest, and remnants can be seen on the island in the middle of Loch Assynt, where the sheep could not get at it. Further north still, past the villages of Scourie and Kinlochbervie – the latter a successful fishing port – the hills have names like Arkle and Foinaven, familiar to the turf, for this is land owned by the Westminster estates and the Duchess named her horses after her mountains. Bending round Loch Eriboll, the road runs east to Tongue and thence to Thurso. Here, the last of the Sutherland hills, Ben Hope and Ben Loyal, look down over the great flatness of the Caithness moorland. There is little sign of habitation amongst these rolling acres, save for the occasional mound of abandoned stones, a bothy or a boathouse.

122

LOW TIDE, OLDSHOREMORE BAY, KINLOCHBERVIE, SUTHERLAND, HIGHLAND.

124

SUILVEN AND LOCH SIONASCAIG FROM STAC POLLAIDH, INVERPOLLY FOREST, HIGHLAND.

LIATACH AND BEINN EIGHE, LOCH CLAIR, GLEN TORRIDON, HIGHLAND.

BEN AN EOIN AND STAC POLLAIDH, INVERPOLLY FOREST, HIGHLAND.

THE FORCAN RIDGE AND THE SADDLE FROM SGURR NA SGINE, GLENSHEIL FOREST, HIGHLAND.

LOCH TORRIDON AND THE BEINN DAMH FOREST, ROSS & CROMARTY, HIGHLAND.

BEINN GHOBLACH AND GRUINARD BAY FROM LAIDE, HIGHLAND.

SGURR FHUARAN, FIVE SISTERS OF KINTAIL, KINTAIL FOREST, HIGHLAND.

FAOCHAG AND THE NORTH SHEIL RIDGE, KINTAIL FOREST, HIGHLAND.

ISLE OF EIGG, SOUND OF ARISAIG, MOIDART, HIGHLAND.

AN TEALLACH: SGURR FIONA AND LORD BERKELEY'S SEAT, DUNDONNELL FOREST, HIGHLAND.

144

SLIOCH, LOCH MAREE, LETTEREWE FOREST, HIGHLAND.

CUL BEAG AND STAC POLLAIDH, INVERPOLLY NATURE RESERVE, HIGHLAND.

FIONAVEN SHROUDED IN MIST, SUTHERLAND, HIGHLAND.

148

THE ISLANDS.

'NOT TO KNOW THE ISLANDS,' said Hugh MacDiarmid, 'is like having a blunt sensation in the tip of your fingers.' There cannot be many travellers in the Hebrides who would disagree. This journey takes us from the Butt of Lewis in the north to the Sound of Gigha in the south, and in between there is an enormous variety of geology, vegetation, animal life – and social conditions. Ownership is perhaps an even more burning issue here than elsewhere in the Highlands, because to maintain an island economy requires consistency and dedication, and many of the maverick purchasers who have decided down the years that owning an island would be fun, or a shrewd investment, are short of both. Depopulation is still the greatest threat to the islands. Here, man does not affect his surroundings because of the weight of his numbers, but because of a lack of them.

Lewis is the northern part of a double island, the largest in Britain, with Harris as its southern end. The basic rock of which it is formed is ancient, and over the years it has been ice-worn into domes and ridges, with deep valleys and fjords on the east, and long stretches of sand and machair on the west. 'This is the oldest land in Europe,' wrote Compton Mackenzie; '. . . the hills of Harris have been so long above the sea as to make parvenus of the Alps.' The highest peak is the Clisham in Harris, which is over 2600 feet. Though the waters of the Minch have been fished to destruction over the years, the town of Stornoway is still an important port, and while crofting these days is a border-line activity, it is still widely practised throughout the island, as is the weaving which produces the famous Harris tweed. This is peat country, and the deposits all over the island can be as deep as 15 feet, producing a fuel which compares well with coal in its output of thermal energy. Many thousands of acres have been successfully converted to grassland. Harris, by contrast, is an island of lochs and mountains, wildly beautiful, a mecca for tourists and anglers, but with a less resilient economy than Lewis. The island of Scalpay, however, to the south, supports a fishing community, and yet further south, Berneray, which is close to the shore of North Uist, is also thriving.

North Uist is the most northerly of a pendant of islands, with Benbecula, South Uist and Barra its southern string. It is a long, low-lying island, with hills to the north and east and a mass of lochs in the interior. There is a nature reserve owned by the RSPB which is home to the rare red-necked phalarope and many other species including the corncrake and the corn bunting. Benbecula, the stepping-stone between North and South Uist, is connected by bridge and causeway to both islands, so there is now a through route from Pollachar in South Uist to Berneray in the north. The airport on Benbecula is an equally important economic and social lifeline. South Uist has the characteristic west-coast sand and machair, with high hills down its spine, and boggy moorland on the eastern side. Its three long sea-lochs, Skiport, Eynort and Boisdale, almost sever it.

Finally, Barra is the most westerly inhabited island in Great Britain, and certainly one of the most beautiful, with great cliffs and sandy bays, wild moorland and long stretches of machair, the sandy flatlands which support a profusion of flowers in the spring. As with the remainder of the Outer Hebrides, remoteness – and the weather – have been the great protectors against the erosion of mass tourism. The number of visitors grows steadily, but these are still islands where solitude can be easily guaranteed – all too easily, in the eyes of some.

The same could not be said of Skye, lying some 15 miles to the east, and a magnet for the modern tourist. The twenty-four rock peaks of the Cuillin Hills are constantly climbed by experts and amateurs alike, and seem hardy enough to resist the worst of the erosion to be found elsewhere. The hills of Trotternish, to the north, and the island of Raasay to the east, with its rich soil and its lush grassland, are still places to be explored in peace, and in the south-west corner, to walk by Loch Scavaig to Loch Coruisk, round the bay of Camusunary, is an act of relative solitude. Most visitors prefer the eastern route, from Broadford north to Portree, whose harbour is a delight. Some will go on to view the astonishing rock outcrop of the Old Man of Storr just north of Portree. Further on, past the little crofting township of Staffin, is the Quirang, a dramatic canyon of grey rock and black pinnacles, with a table of flat turf on top. The western spur of road, which divides at Sligachan in the heart of Skye, takes one to Dunvegan, seat of the Macleods of Macleod, and on to Waternish.

To the south of Skye, Rum, now a nature reserve, is a mountainous island of red Torridon sandstone, with a plunging coastline, and several peaks over 2000 feet, the highest being Askival at 2652 feet. It must always have been a difficult island to farm, and it has had a history of emigration and depopulation. The great exodus of its people took place in 1826 when about 400 of the inhabitants emigrated to America, leaving fewer than 130 people behind. The island was turned over to a herd of 8000 sheep which steadily transformed the vegetation of the island. Today it is inhabited only by employees of Scottish Natural Heritage – it was acquired by SNH's predecessor, the Nature Conservancy, in 1957. A scattering of houses at the pierhead is dominated by Kinloch Castle, an Edwardian extravaganza, the interior of which has remained virtually unchanged since the turn of the century, and which now acts both as a hostel for visitors and a luxury hotel. Rum is a naturalist's dream. There are golden eagles, a herd of some 1500 red deer, a small colony of wild goats, and the famous wild Rum ponies. Close study of the deer has shown a deterioration in their quality since sheep and cattle were removed from the island. The lack of manuring and the coarsening of the grass appear to have had a severe effect on the grazing. However, the study of an island deprived of a viable population has yielded valuable information about how to restore a vegetation which has suffered from over-grazing and burning.

Canna, to the west of Rum, a green and fertile island, was once the herring centre of the Hebrides, its natural harbour offering shelter to hundreds of vessels. More recently it has seen its population fall to a level which at present is fewer than twelve. It has owed its survival as an island crofted in the traditional manner to the enlightened ownership of Dr John Lorne Campbell, whose knowledge of Gaelic language and culture is legendary. It was well tended over the forty-three years that he and his wife owned it, with dikes maintained, ditches dug and trees planted. In 1981 it was gifted to the Scottish National Trust whose task it now is to ensure that Canna has a viable future, for crofting, as a place for visitors, perhaps for Gaelic and archaeological studies and for naturalists.

To the south-east of Canna, beyond Rum, lies Eigg with its distinctive Scuir standing out like a natural sphinx, overlooking 7000 acres of relatively low ground. For much of the present century it was owned by the Runciman family who maintained it as a farming island with a small population of around 130. Today it is the property of Yorkshire-born Keith Shellenberg, and though conditions on the island have deteriorated over the years, his intention is to restore its fortunes. The tiny island of Muck, to the south of Eigg, has three families on it, with the redoubtable McEwans of Muck still making a living there.

South to Mull, Coll and Tiree, three islands of differing fortunes and geology. Mull is volcanic, with its highest peak, Ben More, standing at 3170 feet. In the south, at Carsaig, there is a very English-looking chalk-stream with water-cress – one of only two in the Highlands. Elsewhere the ground is more rugged. Despite the fact that it is relatively rich agriculturally, Mull's indigenous population has fallen over the years to fewer than 2000, though in summer its cottages are let and tourists throng the place. The holy island of Iona to the south-west is a strong attraction for visitors. Coll, to the east, is low-lying, its highest peak no more than 340 feet, with fine sandy beaches and good grazing on the machair. It supports a farming rather than a crofting community, since in the last century, Ayrshire farmers were asked to take over the land after a clearance, but its present population is only about 150. Tiree is even flatter, but is a place of great charm and beauty, with silver beaches and green grassland, supporting a population of around 1000.

Jura, to the south, means, in Gaelic, 'deer island' and it has had a long history as a place for hunting. In the southern part of the island the Paps of Jura rise to 2571 feet, from where, on a good day, you can see from the Cuillins in the north to the Isle of Man in the south. The west of the island is wild, trackless and devoid of human habitation. Elsewhere, crofting and a newly built distillery support a population of around 250 people. Perhaps the most famous physical feature of Jura is the fearsome tidal race of Corriebhreacan, running between Jura and the island of Scarba. It is officially deemed unnavigable, with a speed of eight knots and only fifteen minutes of slack water time.

Islay is the largest island of the Inner Hebrides, a place of green, arable land and peat, used to prepare its famous malt whiskies. Its three main townships support a population of around 4000, and though its proximity to Glasgow has meant a steady drain of people away from the island over the years, the balance of tourism, farming and distilling, together with smaller local industries, has made Islay a reasonably settled place. The same cannot, alas, be said for Gigha, which lies between Islay and the Mull of Kintyre. Here, for years, Sir James Horlick, of malted milk fame, attended to a small but contented population of around 190 people. He encouraged dairy farming, created a superb garden of rhododendrons, and encouraged the introduction of regular water and electricity supplies. Today, after several changes of ownership, the future is less certain. As with so many of the islands of the west, there is a need on Gigha for an owner who is prepared to invest, not just money but time and energy for its people and its future. The fragile economy of the Hebrides needs constant protection, whether it is lobbying for better transport links, campaigning for grants, or seeing that the interests of crofters or fishermen are properly represented in council chambers, in Edinburgh or at Westminster.

If this section has concentrated on people rather than on the natural ecology of the land, that is because on the islands of the west, man rather than nature is the endangered species, and man, properly equipped, is what gives the land hope for the future. Deserted islands may have a certain fascination for the convinced romantic, but, deprived of human habitation, they become what Frank Fraser Darling called 'devastated terrain', wilderness areas perhaps, but without the balance of man and nature which is the ideal state. Here there is actually a need for more rather than less tourism, seasonal though that may be. However distasteful it may be for the purist to contemplate coach-loads of trippers pouring over the hallowed turf of Iona or clogging the foothills of the Cuillins, and however sad it may be to count the number of holiday cottages, owned by outsiders and deserted during the winter months, it would be worse for the local economy without them. The alternatives are hard to find. What is needed, through the various agencies and institutions responsible for the needs of the Highlands and Islands, is a state of constant watchfulness.

'Do not be deluded!' wrote Hugh MacDiarmid. 'There is nothing here but just a lot of water and rocks. Just a lot of water and rocks – peace and beauty and the glories of an ancient people.'

SUNSET OVER PEAT-BOGS, ISLE OF ISLAY, STRATHCLYDE.

THE CUILLIN RIDGE FROM ELGOL, ISLE OF SKYE, HIGHLAND.

Bruach na Frithe, Coire na Creiche, Glen Brittle, Isle of Skye, Highland.

THE OLD MAN OF STORR AND SATELLITES AND THE ISLE OF RAASAY, ISLE OF SKYE, HIGHLAND.

THE QUIRAING FROM THE STORR AT DAWN, ISLE OF SKYE, HIGHLAND.

Bidean Druim na Ramh and Sgurr an Fheadain, Coire na Creiche, Glen Brittle, Isle of Skye, Highland.

164

TWILIGHT, BROADFORD BAY, ISLE OF SKYE, HIGHLAND.

166

SEA SPRAY ON BASALT COLUMNS, ISLE OF STAFFA, HIGHLAND.

168

BEN MORE, LOCH NA KEAL, ISLE OF MULL, HIGHLAND.

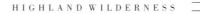

LICHENS AND BOULDER, BEN MORE, ISLE OF MULL, HIGHLAND.

ARDNARMURCHAN POINT FROM MISHNISH, ISLE OF MULL, HIGHLAND.

174

SRON SCOURST, GLEN MEAVAIG AND THE FOREST OF HARRIS, ISLE OF HARRIS, WESTERN ISLES.

176

FOREST OF HARRIS FROM TRAIGH ROSAMOL, LUSKENTYRE, ISLE OF HARRIS, WESTERN ISLES.

TRAIGH SEILEBOST FROM TRAIGH LUSKENTYRE, ISLE OF HARRIS, WESTERN ISLES.

180

Loch na Cleavag, Cravadale, Isle of Harris, Western Isles.

Traigh Nisabost, Sound of Taransay, Isle of Harris, Western Isles.

184

Ben Hiant, Morven Peninsula, Sound of Mull, Isle of Mull, Highland.

THE PAPS OF JURA FROM FORELAND, ISLE OF ISLAY, STRATHCLYDE.

BLAVEN AND LOCH CILL CHRIOSD, ISLE OF SKYE, HIGHLAND.

MOONRISE, SGURR NAN GOBHAR, CUILLINS, ISLE OF SKYE, HIGHLAND.

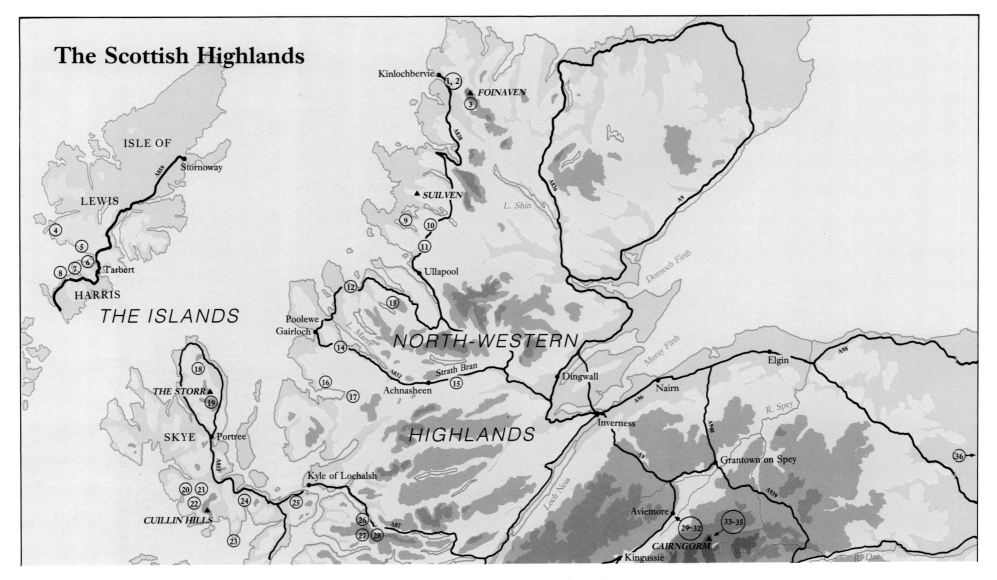

The Scottish Highlands

Kinlochbervie

① 1, 2
▲ *FOINAVEN*
③

A838

ISLE OF
• Stornoway

LEWIS

▲ *SUILVEN*

④

⑨ ⑩

⑤

⑪

⑦ ⑥
⑧ ⑦ • Tarbert

Ullapool

HARRIS

⑫

THE ISLANDS

⑬

Poolewe
Gairloch

⑭

NORTH-WESTERN

L. Maree

A832

Strath Bran

⑯ Achnasheen ⑮

⑰

HIGHLANDS

⑱

THE STORR ▲
⑲

SKYE • Portree

A855

⑳ ㉑

Kyle of Lochalsh

㉒

CUILLIN HILLS ㉔

㉓

㉕

㉖
A87
㉗ ㉘

L. Shin

A836

A9

Dornoch Firth

Moray Firth

• Elgin

A98

Dingwall

• Nairn

A96

Inverness

Loch Ness

A9

Grantown on Spey

A939

Aviemore •

㉙–㉜ ㉝–㉟

CAIRNGORM
Kingussie

R. Spey

R. Dee

㊱

Numbers on the map refer to the approximate location of each photograph and are referred to their respective page number below:

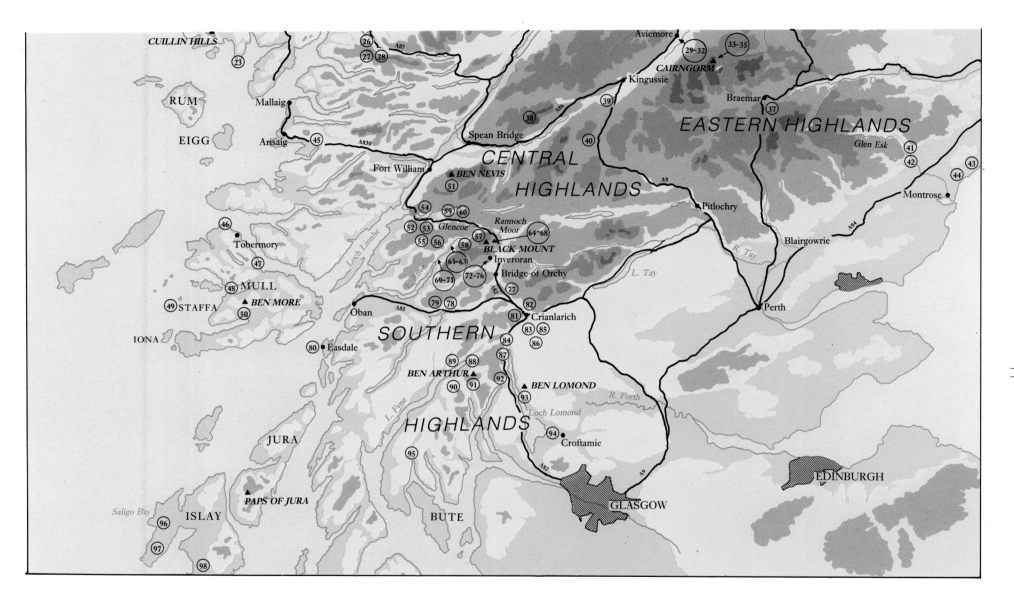

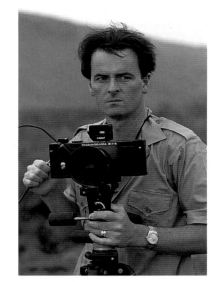

190

PHOTOGRAPHIC NOTE. LANDSCAPE PHOTOGRAPHY for me is a very personal pursuit. The photographs within this book are the result of my own attempts to be at one with the natural world. It is always moving to witness a spectacular natural event in a wild place, and when this experience is focused through the lens of the camera I find myself in resonance with nature.

The challenge facing the landscape photographer is to capture these rare moments on film. I see my part as a photographic medium, through which the events pass and are recorded for others to share. My aim is to depict images of land and instants of emotional intensity.

My own 'thumb print' is of course evident in the images — as a photographer, I am responsible for selecting the composition, exposure, time of day and film type which best enhance each occasion. A good landscape photograph is a combination of three separate elements: technical proficiency, fine light and an identifiable personal vision.

The camera used for the photographs in this book was the Linhof 617S — a specialized panoramic camera, highly regarded by professionals for its precise design, its superb optics and its accurate viewfinder. Utilizing roll film, it produces four shots on a single roll of 120 film and unlike some panoramic cameras the lens is non-rotational, delivering distortion-free results from its fixed Schneider Super Angulon 90mm f5.6. In addition the Schneider centre-spot neutral density filter was used in all images to ensure that even exposure was achieved throughout the format (a reduction of two stops is necessary). A tripod was used in all cases. Normal camera settings were generally between 1 and 1/4S, f16.5 and f45, to maximize depth of field.

Film stock is a combination of Fuji RFP 50 and Fuji Velvia RVP 50, which I now use extensively. Velvia has exceeded my own expectations, delivering extraordinary colour saturation and brilliance with unparalleled sharpness. Its granularity rating is 9, similar to that of Kodachrome 25; however it is one stop faster, is E6 compatible and can therefore be pushed/pulled in processing. It is a marked improvement over RFP with a rating of 11 – Kodachrome 64 falls between them, at 10.

At the end of some chapters are images taken with both Hasselblad and Nikon equipment. For most landscape work, I have found 35mm disappointing in both image reproduction and quality. Similarly with Hasselblad equipment, whilst the larger format and superior optics are superb, I have found the square format undesirable for landscape work – for someone who visualizes in panoramic format, a square has no capacity to deliver the visualized image.

For many years I wrestled with formats and maintain that they are an overlooked aspect of photographic visualization. 617 is for me the perfect landscape format because it complements the way I see the world. With a format ratio of 3:1 and a fixed 90mm lens, a photographer has the ability to create spectacular images.

Like most other things in life it doesn't come without its disadvantages – the most significant being that an image must be found which works with the format and this generally takes a good deal of searching out. In this respect the format is restrictive and persistence is required to achieve consistent results. Furthermore, conditions generally have to be optimum to utilize the camera's full potential and, unlike conventional camera systems, the ability to use interchangeable lenses and thus create a variety of images in any given location is not available to the panoramic photographer.

I recently began using a 612 format – the camera a Linhof 612PC II fitted with a Schneider Super Augulon 65mm f5.6 which has the added features of perspective control and interchangeable lenses. The camera employs a built in lens rise and has a format ratio of 2:1. It performs in situations where the limitations of 617 are exceeded, e.g. shooting high mountains from a low glen or photographing a tall forest from a boat. The format is complementary to 617, but is distinctly different.

Highland Wilderness is a portfolio of some of the wildest landscapes, not only in Scotland but in the world. Some wilderness areas are a direct result of remoteness and small populations and have remained with their flora and fauna in their natural state, with little disturbance from man. With more leisure time, improved access by road and vehicles and technological advances in outdoor equipment these areas are now vulnerable and I would urge anyone inspired by the images in this book to take nothing but pictures and leave nothing but footprints.

COLIN PRIOR 1992

ACKNOWLEDGEMENTS

I am indebted to my father for his unrelenting support throughout this project – particularly during the winter months on some of the 'big shoots', when the weight of ice equipment is an additional burden.

My thanks also go to Bob MacDonald and the staff at Graham Tiso, Glasgow for their helpful advice and assistance; to Linhof Professional Sales for their technical expertise and backup and finally to my family for allowing my frequent absences.